THE NEW TOURISM

for Maggie —

" Where are my glasses?
No end to wonder. "

with much love,

Harry

THE NEW TOURISM

HARRY MATHEWS

SAND PAPER PRESS

KEY WEST

THE NEW TOURISM
ISBN 978-0-9843312-3-9
Copyright © 2010 by Harry Mathews

Several poems herein have been previously published, sometimes in different form: "Butter and Eggs: a didactic poem" in *Boston Review* and *The Best American Poetry* (2002); "First Love at First Sight," "The White Wind," and "Tinguely Museum 8/27/06" in *PN Review* (U.K.); "In Praise of Heinrich Heine," "Romantic Poem," and "Sussex Days" in both *PN Review* and *The Sienese Shredder*; "Ptyx" in *Marginalia: A Journal of Innovative Literature* and *Accident créateur* (Paris); "Lateral Disregard" in *Jacket, Shiny,* and *The Best American Poetry* (2004); "Waiting for Dusk" in *Golden Handcuffs*; and "Crème Brûlée" in *Detroit, i.e. Infrastructure.* A selection from "Haikus before sleep" was published as *Day Shifts* (Brussels). "The New Tourism," "Genoa as Rendezvous," "In Pursuit of Henry Vaughan," and "I know that my redeemer liveth" are published synchronously with this edition in *Maggy*.

This book was designed for Sand Paper Press by David Janik in Los Angeles, California. The text is set in Bauer Bodoni. Title pages are set in Hypatia Sans Pro.

SAND PAPER PRESS
716 LOVE LANE
KEY WEST
FLORIDA
33040

sandpaperpress.net

To Ann Beattie & Lincoln Perry

I

II

III

I

Butter and Eggs: a didactic poem

1

The circular cast-iron skillet, used for nothing else, is an eighth of an inch thick
and broad enough to let its contents spread unhindered.

The skillet is set over high heat, its cooking surface greased
with a mild oil, or butter cut with oil, or best of all clarified butter, itself pure oil.

Broken into a bowl and salted, two eggs are sprinkled with coarsely chopped parsley and chives,
then beaten roundly with a small fork until they twirl in a ring.

The oiled skillet smokes faintly. The beaten eggs, tipped into its center,
sizzle in a circle that tilting widens as desired.
Joggling the skillet shifts the thickening eggs back and forth and at last
slides them to the rim opposite its handle, where the emerging lip
is flipped with the tip of the fork towards the center of the circle
and rolled back towards its nearer edge. The opposite edges
may not quite fold shut, but any gap is closed
by neatly overturning the contents of the skillet onto a plate.

On the plate the eggs continue to cook,
so a moist interior in the skillet yields a dry interior on the plate
while a moist interior on the plate wants a runny interior in the skillet,
and for a runny interior on the plate the interior in the skillet must be disconcertingly soggy.
These facts are variously modified if, across the circle of newly-poured eggs
(in these cases lacking the speckling of herbs),
mushrooms are aligned, or diced fried lard, or grated tart cheese.

2

Hot water is poured two inches deep into a small pot
that is set covered over a high flame until it boils. The flame is lowered;
a fresh egg, its shell pricked at the rounder end with a medium-fine pin,
is lowered with a spoon into the simmering water; the lid is set back in place.
After four minutes the egg is—at sea level—spooned out and rinsed in cold water;
at higher altitudes, allowance is made for the progressively lower temperatures
at which water boils: ten seconds is added for every thousand feet.
In Santa Fe an egg is not cooked in less than five minutes.

The egg may be broken into a bowl, then buttered and salted;
or set in an egg cup, small end up, in which case the shell
is circularly crackled by tapping with the back of a knife
half an inch below the tip, then opened with a thrust of the blade.
Salting should be restrained but never omitted, as the French maxim implies:
"A kiss without a moustache is like an egg without salt."
A spoon of wood or plastic leaves the savor intact.

3

In a tall three-quart pot, two quarts of water are brought to a boil.
A tablespoon of vinegar is added. The water is stirred with the spoon
in a strong circular stroke that spins it against the sides of the pot
so as to form at its center a vortex whose momentum sustains itself
while an egg is broken into the whirling hollow. Instantly cooked,
the white of the egg enwraps the yolk, restoring a shape
like that of the unbroken shell. Use then determines the time
when the egg must be extracted with a slotted spoon:
whether, dried in paper toweling, it is to be set on a trimmed slice of toast
to be eaten salted, soft, and hot; or, cooled and firm, reserved for immersion
in a ramekin of aspic lined with a thin slice of ham, with two leaves
of blanched tarragon laid crosswise on the congealing stock.

4

A tablespoon of fat—butter, bacon grease, mild oil—is gently warmed
in a small, trustworthy skillet. A lid that can seal the skillet
is placed directly on another flame, set high. Two eggs are broken
into the warmed skillet, with care not to rupture the yolks,
and moderately seasoned with salt and pepper. When the lid
is too hot to touch, it is set over the eggs
and from time to time briefly removed to observe them:
patience and attentiveness are both required
to seize the moment of perfection
when the whites are no longer glairy,
the yolks not yet whitening,
and the eggs are tilted (unstuck if needs be with a rubber spatula)
at once out of the skillet onto the breakfast plate.

5

A tablespoon of oil, bacon grease, or clarified butter
is heated in a medium or large skillet set on the highest possible flame.
Broken into a bowl, two eggs seasoned with salt and pepper
are briefly but strenuously beaten. When the fat sizzles and smokes
at maximum heat, the skillet is withdrawn from the flame,
the eggs are poured into its center and there with a fork or wooden spatula
immediately stirred and turned so that no part of them
stays long in contact with the scorching surface but the whole
is uninterruptedly mixed and remixed until, attaining a soft solidity,
it can be folded upon itself and promptly flipped onto a plate.
Scarcely ten seconds pass between the moment the eggs
touch the skillet and their removal. The flame should be extinguished.

6

Eight quarter-pound sticks of sweet butter are pressed
into a two-quart double boiler or bain-marie
that is brought to a boil and kept simmering
while the butter softens slowly into a muddled yellowish soup
that gradually separates on three levels: floating at the top,
a layer of foamy casein; a residuum of casein settling
on the bottom; and between them a depth
of clear oil of butter. When these strata are stable,
the flame is extinguished and the upper pot
removed slowly and surely to a counter where it rests
until the casein layers have steadied. The froth
is then skimmed off with a spoon or tea strainer,
and with surpassing gentleness the butter oil is poured
into a jar. The operation may need to be performed
more than once to keep the underlying casein
from slithering over the rim of the pot while one salvages
every possible drop of oil, which afterwards—except
for what is of immediate use—is sealed in its container
and refrigerated. This perfect cooking butter
will not turn rancid and, heated to high temperatures,
never brown or burn: it is the word "blessing" clarified.

II

First Love at First Sight

for M. A. S.

Stupefaction of flounced white organdy
I was already dazed crossing the palatial room
Then a dazing smile, too, studded with blue braces
Like lead bullets in a white bandolier.
It was all over, or I was.
(Some years later, a few fox-trots.)
That was before bedskirts and foie gras,

When I could write. Did I talk about the immolation scene
Or *The Constant Nymph*? Or play it dumb as I was?
It hasn't been leitmotifs that bring you to mind,
You're a lost idea, although I wonder if hair now tinted blonde
Droops on slender bones, and what you are reading,
The Nutmeg of Consolation perhaps, or *Brand New Cherry Flavor*.

The New Tourism

Where is it I came from
And where is it I'm stranded?
Part of the maps is black
And the rest's in borrowed language.

I have nothing to wear
And shops won't take my money.
Kids have buckled my knees
And blear has filled my eyelids.

Iron lips are slick
And burning books are sunny
But I can't see the point
Of the busy wizened creatures.

Why think of fear
At placid foreign features?
Strangest are the tears
Of the busy wizened creatures.

Where is it I came from
And where is it I'm stranded?
Part of the maps is black
And the rest's in borrowed language.

In Praise of Heinrich Heine

In longing, the underage seaman veered from the drift;
Elsewhere, out of the wind, scuppered his stone desire.
Unluck cleaving to him made him no schadenfreudiger—
What was plus or minus? He loved the least cat.

Starbursts should light up this moment, the child
Be jealous of nighttime and its laughing yellow listener!
The red doe of the prince of studies sunders,
Shedding her likeness, and her undimmed luster fits him.

The White Wind

No doubt you are like me, wanting what we look for.
Perhaps you are not like me, unable to go on.
Unsuccess having so worn me out
I feel I'm about to lose everything,
Thinking of that one object
Always just out of hope of reach
Makes me want to stop and sit down.
It's like catching the wind in a net.
You who are like me, can believe me:
Waste your time as well as I,
Spelled on the girdle of your longing
You will read in plain diamond letters,
"I belong to powers beyond you.
I wriggle out of all possession
With a smile on my fangs."

Romantic Poem

for L. S.

In the dead of night
In the dead of the past
The landscape of mathematical bats
With inviting slate-lined troughs sunk in gravel
Can you think of me
Can you think of us
Armorially entangled like a bunch of bananas
In wastelands of utopian desire
Can you think
How can real things if lovable be so uncomfortable
Sloth, nevermindness, sweetish pus
Excuses worse than astrological babble
Tomorrow was another day
With vicious sunlight
Not even room enough to moralize
Just get down and stay down
I can't remember but then you
Are not to be forgotten
Putting myself out of your reach
Backing towards immobility
So sluggishly attained
Then as now

Genoa as Rendezvous

At Accrod's: our obligatory
solitary playground.
Across cratered coal dust
a dented leaden foot-
ball bounds stodgily
towards movable poles
of variable goals—
a grabyard of remembrances!
I went looking
for a safe hiding place
and a stump of candle
to recall a once-upon-a-time
Genoese lunch
where we began
forgiving one another
and ourselves
never too soon.

Ptyx

Send all our sleds across the ice
Six miles north to Elysium
Where cedar clouds break on the stone
And the sun it raineth every day.

Erotic strife was never so pure
As to leave no cranny where love might creep
And curl itself up until next night;
For the sun it raineth every day.

Lateral Disregard

after an observation by Kenneth Koch

Shall I compare thee to a summer's bay
an orange cliff rising from its waters to the east
to the west a slope of reddish earth whorled with gray olives
between them an arc of rock, then sand, then a little port
four houses of blue-washed rubble and red-tile roofs
and below them under broad-leaved vines a terrace with tables and benches
from which at noon the smoke of golden bream grilling
brings a gust of longing to the wayfarer as he looks over the bay
from a bluff down which a dusty zigzag path
leads to a straggly cluster of fig trees near the water's edge
(their first fruits now ripened in July sun)
to whose left on flat rocks ample nets have been drying
to whose right on the sand—green, yellow, green, red—four fishing craft
rest through the languid hours of the blue day
only at night taking to the clear dark waters
through which their bow-lights beckon curious fish
for nets to scoop from their nimble careers
to be shaken over the decks in slithering heaps
and at dawn the boats coast home between brighter blues
the glory of the world suffuses earth stone and leaf
land and sea reaffirm their distinction
in an exchange so gentle that the wayfarer briefly believes
he has been suspended lastingly in newborn light
no longer dreaming plowing on through thick mud?

Sussex Days

Singing sheds its sound,
Soundless song is articulated
In mauve fevers
Stinging the unopened nose.

Halal lamb is distributed
Like goose on Christmas afternoon.
You are likewise cut into pieces, relics
Suitable for passionate sleepiness.

Tinguely Museum 8/27/06

"This door is no internal door, please keep clear
And follow the green seven-link snake
By the seat of your pants
To the other end of town, the temple of cellar slides
Into fluid darkness, where your lost friend
And his paramour evolve
In retroactive determination to escape
Your deserving arms, and to accomplish wonders
That define their death, a fluid death
That you cannot retrieve, nor will you
When this pen runs dry
And you with it."

No Regrets, Though

Remember in the old days when we used to share a garage
And even sometimes each other's car or two?
We talked a lot, flirted some.
I'm writing this because I like remembering
Your class, your looks, mercies in themselves.
I won't go on about that, no talent for it,
But tell me about the cars, they say you're into new ones now.
Do you still have the great old Packard? It's unforgettable,
That old Packard, you can't beat it, don't let it go.
It takes off like a racehorse, purrs like a pussy
When you go for broke, turns tough corners, not even a wobble.
Take it out against the others, it'll leave them at the gate,
Ride them into the ditch, spin them into the far lane,
Bash them without a scratch, bust their radiators.
Better that than your flashing around in them yourself.
People say you're a glam scavenger looking for trouble—
You should save that stuff for nighttime or another county.
Keep your savvy up front and make the old guy happy.
I don't like your being talked about, not like that.

In Pursuit of Henry Vaughan

Can we, can I remember happiness?
Do I know when I'm happy, except when it's over?
And is there an original happiness that I can look back to,
at a time when I'd learned how to eat
and not yet learned how to write?
Later, of course, letters became the source
of another happiness, one that unlike
the happiness of illiteracy removed me from where I was.

If I knew I had lost that first happiness,
I knew it could never be recovered.
I don't think I bothered to try, I was then busy
attending to all the things that meanwhile were going wrong.
I felt I had gone wrong myself, that I myself
had made this happen: a conviction
that brought me only the certainties of remorse.
I misread what was happening around me,
misunderstood what was said; I swallowed food without tasting it,
even shut my nose as though it were an offending eye;
I spoke stupidly to available friends; I took refuge
in mental dreams and solitary lechery;
and the proof of my wrongdoing
erupted in my face for all to see. Every mirror
confirmed that I was an affront to the world.
I attained my teenage acme.

Attentions of others helped me dilute

this self-disgust, but I have never renounced it entirely;
and I cannot sometimes help regretting
my youngest years when I did not know *m* from *e*.
My few words then were my own. From the branches of a red maple
into which I used to climb, the world spread vastly
in a summer that included me. From my perch,
the houses I saw were cool and welcoming—
they remain so today, but when I enter them
my thoughts have wandered elsewhere. Perhaps later,
in my last moments, I can choose to relent
and, however briefly, recover that undoubting ignorance
(all its bad dreams effaced)
that I so cleverly abandoned.

Waiting for Dusk

Whoever in the span of his life is confronted by the word "pomegranate"
will experience a mixture of feelings: a longing to see at least once the face
of a Mediterranean god or nymph or faun; the memory of an old silver mirror
decorated with images of varied fruits; a regret at never having known the spell
of a summer picnic ending with the taste of acrid seeds spat over the bridge
parapet—you look down at your scarlet-stained fingers and up at the weather

of the sky as it changes (a black thunderhead, a blue depth), thinking of the same weather
crossing centuries and landscapes. I don't know whether I like the pomegranate
as food or dislike it; perhaps neither, thinking of it more as a bridge
to other, lost lives. But here now is Simon, with his smiling silly face
from which he extracts tough seeds from his teeth with one awkward forefinger, a spell
of not unsympathetic bad manners that, if truth be told, is a mirror

of our own, perhaps more furtive acts. Then he puts on his mask, made of mirror-
like chromed metal, and I think, why, he could face and kill Medusa! Any weather
has its charm, even the green tempest surrounding her writhing snakes that spell
death to the unwary traveler, snakes like a wreath of leeks in a Dutch still life where a pomegranate
cut in two glows idly near the table edge. I stroll with Simon, averting my eyes from his face,
on the path that leads down to the edge of the stream and the pool under the bridge

where fanged pike lie deep among bearded stones. The pillars and vaults of the bridge
rise sturdily above us and are completed into wavering ellipses in the mirror
of the slow-moving water. This is a moment between here and there, between the face
of worldly things and their unstable reflections which in the basically sunny weather
suggest reveries tending to sleep, and then sadness. Remember the pomegranate
sliced on the unvarnished table, I tell myself, that's something sharp and real! But the spell

of the season and the melancholy hour, sweetened and damped with wine, spell
another evolution of my afternoons of regrets, far from the Mediterranean and the bridge
at Pisa, far from the land of Nordic dream where the lemon and the pomegranate
drop irregular sweet-and-sour globes on slopes scented and dry that are the dusky mirror
of a life so seemingly simple that we think of even the treacherous weather
as a seamless warm continuum of sun, moon, and stars. I know that I know better, I try to face

my life here, with Simon: he has taken off his mask; it has left on his face
a stripe or two like accidental marks of his real pain but that in fact spell
nothing but themselves—nothing. He appears relaxed in this comfortable weather,
sauntering ahead of me as we cross back over the wood-in-concrete bridge,
unaware that in the declining light his silly smiling face is the mirror
of my disjunction. The picnic spot is littered with wrecks of pomegranate.

Can my face ever be as actual as a pomegranate?
Will the weather ever settle down? What dumb idea will replace the functioning bridge?
What spell can make the masks of things real? What mirror will reveal them?

Crème brûlée

For me the identification of trees has always been a puzzle, one not really made easier by consulting the tree books inside my house, where no trees are. I can certainly remember the caramel color of beech leaves in fall, the cropped silhouettes of plane trees along the highway, the almost-blue brown trunks of fallen spruces I've had to cross over or skirt on my walks, the purpled boughs of Judas trees where no swallow ever perches.

But do swallows ever perch? It seems that every swallow I've seen out of its caked nest is part of an ever-changing, bug-eating swarm—a puzzle too mobile to decipher, tumbling and soaring over the cross of a church in Tuscany or Touraine, with pink evening light inside the bell of the air, an image that saddens me when I return to a highway leading north into the night thick and empty as caramel custard. But of course *crème brûlée* is the new name for caramel custard, and probably a new name was needed, because before you swallow any custard you now have to crack through a delicious crust, something that on the highway may stir your desire to drive on to your next restaurant. Restaurants are a puzzle in themselves: how far is the next good one you can reach before you step inside the hospitable, softly lit walls?

Through an entrance lined with vases full of leaves and flowers, you cross to a room full of tables, sumptuously or plainly set, sometimes a cross between the two. But by this time you have abandoned every thought of caramel anything. You are now interested by what is to be found inside the menu, inside the wine list. You order and wait and meanwhile have a first swallow of the local white, of a denomination you don't have to puzzle your head over. You soon forget about having to drive along the highway, the hard driving you already had to do, with lights on the far side of the highway making you tense slightly (and when undimmed making you slightly cross).

You reflect as the wine mellows you that if life is a puzzle, travel is another. Why ever leave your house, why leave behind the caramel-colored leaves and the bluish brown trunks? Take another swallow and enjoy it. Let the sweet melancholy of wine expel the demons inside you.

There are no demons inside you, just your addiction to any puzzle that will addle your contentment, like salt in caramel. You swallow your last glass of wine and return, not unhappily, to the highway.

I know that my redeemer liveth

Why Susie, please stay—
A centripetal bird
That's threading the maze
In the chowdown space

May prop up your stool
Of slitted sticks
Or her black parted beak
Turn your red rash pink.

Haikus Before Sleep

No bizarre tulips
Can link distant parallels
In needed madness.

What hands, and how used,
What oils, what poems released
In my son's body?

Things hard to endure:
A woman I love scolds me;
Dinner badly served.

Dead eyes look through me.
After a sweetheart's scolding,
Her eyes look past me.

The beloved leaves.
Later, friends laugh together.
Later, song, then pain.

Forgetting twice. *Twice.*
Lacings; white lilacs blooming;
Old friends, new contexts.

Oysters would have helped.
Neither they nor golden bream
Were for sale today.

Works done with pleasure?
Levers of melancholy
Skew my peopled streets.

I think I should cry.
Laura consistently smiles.
I'm stuck in a craze.

Does having things work
Spoil the want of poetry?
Haiku forgotten.

My beloved friend
Who swears that he is happy
Is perhaps living.

Good wine brings the friends?
The friend enchanted the wine—
A friend at last mine.

After country, crowd.
Country rain smells of rotting,
City rain of stone.

Late lunch for late friends.
Drunk all afternoon, writing.
Friends save strange late wine.

I was waiting for
A satisfying likeness.
It came. Then: ego!

Furtive images,
Swallows shrill, no swallows seen.
But kind relatives.

Body work. Much time
But little to show for it.
I am the virgin.

The sky's blue and far,
Sadness stalking passively.
She says, "Let it go."

Coming home: from what?
How to define a fullness
Where I did nothing?

Trowel in soft earth
Is not gentler than a son
Disarming words feared.

Morning so distant.
Since then, sweetest food, wine work,
And old friends sweetest.

The summons of wine
Enlivens and cripples me:
An alcoholic.

Clear sky. New glasses
To unnerve me with clearness.
Less winy madness.

Pure sunlight darkens.
Travel must now be prepared.
Into what weather?

"Although I'm reeling—"…
Byron cannot help me now,
Although I am, too.

"2:30 a.m."
I must be Frank O'Hara,
Or a disciple.

The woman with me
Smells elder quicker than I.
Blooms stinking with life.

Hay threshed and removed.
No thing hurt in the process;
Not cows, grass, or me.

At the end of day
Unparalleled perspective:
The marble-lost clouds.

Words, garden, music,
All with my clumsy green thumbs.
What is happiness?

First words are set down,
Setting memory, not truth:
Today's birds and dung.

No sun in the sky.
A vine explodes in the house.
The rain keeps falling.

Frost in mid-July
(At night, of course, and not much)
Is a reminder.

More rain, but a walk.
Comings and goings; reading.
Wagner! An orchid.

"My wife loves me less."
"Light blue and gold"—odd and true,
With immanent tears.

37

The rain like a shroud,
one that enfolded us both.
Who missed the brief sun?

The living and dead
constitute one memory:
scissored wall lettuce.

Both friends have left us,
one traveling north, one south.
Mist blurs weeded soil.

Where is the roofer?
The rain drips through my wiring
electrically.

Così fan tutte
is the purple clematis
on the wall called death.

Sky is all today.
The sky is following me.
Nonsense, says the drink.

A six-year-old boy
looks at me as someone real.
No time for fuckups.

How write a haiku
on a Japanese evening?
There was my young self.

It is difficult
to know what children forget.
Rain: falling asleep.

No time for some things,
but plotting a French sonnet
makes my ears wake up.

My nails are warping,
my knees have no cartilage—
sunset: mauve, orange.

No walking today—
bell flowers small and smaller,
the great bird frightened.

I knew him aged five.
What frightened the bees away?
And the hive is dead.

Waiting for thunder.
Meanwhile, happy reunions.
Breath-giving stillness.

Has my son returned?
A near-dead root was watered.
The sun will come back.

There is no last word.
Thunder and lightning are gone.
Wine drunk together.

Now ninety years old—
"Why be congratulated?"
I'll hug my ash tree.

Makes one want to cry,
the light like golden music,
Marie's vinaigrette.

Nine days have gone by
since I wrote my last haiku
here: Lans: my haven.

Where are we going?
That at last is decided.
Thunder and lightning.

No hearing, warped sight,
This exquisite traveler.
Her name is my own.

Where are my glasses?
There is no end to wonder.
Pinocchio is glad.

So this day was full,
with not one cause for remorse.
It was too easy.

"There is no haiku,"
a haiku John Ashbery
might have said today.

My poem vanished
into another language
just as it first did.

What a kindly day—
everything taken care of
in brisk autumn wind.

A day of returns—
rain, fog, mountain chilliness,
and walking naked.

Niki's works re-hung.
Facts from the Hundred Years War.
Beech leaves turning "gold."

The sky cleared: regret.
Comforting clouds at noontime.
Fair daughter, blithe son.

Whatever we dance,
music calls another tune,
rain on other graves.

Is this Englishman
a friend—a possible friend?
The bright wheel still turns.

Abergavenny
with four English syllables
(in Welsh, Y Fenni)

deserves two haikus
for making me so happy
with its mists and musts.

Last night (no haiku!)
they said I read with success.
Nights falling early.

Another surprise:
Schumann's Opus 17
brought to new life (mine).

44

The circuit broken,
me perched on a high platform
I learned what dark means.

A mad wind started,
scaring me out of Mozart,
and the roof held tight.

What is happening
cannot be defined by mice;
but mice more than friends.

Strange news of the day:
the big game is still scoreless.
My daughter. My wife.

A card of haikus,
a whole card has disappeared.
(It was not quite full.)

Locking myself out:
a lesson others kept brief.
And *then* doing things.

No haiku tonight.
It's late, I'm falling asleep,
can't count the brown leaves.

What is there to tell
but that remorse is mortal?
Combed fluff of sunset.

At last the wind wanes,
well-being waning with it
then love perking up.

I stoned; what haiku?
"What you want to know, brother?"
Just the hi! of coo.

46

I keep complaining,
says devoted companion.
Something must be wrong!

The unknown vast. This?
Dolphins close enough to hug,
a sure horizon.

A delicious night
after a confusing day.
(Is confusion best?)

From where in the world
is my wife looking at me?
Not under the bed.

It's all in the head,
but my head ends at my toes.
Busy day. Sun. Rest.

Is "head" not "the mind"?
I cannot "work on myself."
Water runs downhill.

Bougainvillea
blazes on our back front yard
that we'd never seen.

I waited too late.
I can't write haikus tonight.
The whiteness is all.

A farewell dinner,
then our guest invited us.
Accept this. Accept.

Only images.
The glories of Italy.
Our tailless lizard.

When a lover lies
I think: trust is made of dust.
Nevertheless: trust.

Sadness and anger
yield to a commerce with friends,
inside, watching rain.

Did I mean "drenching"?
Not very original—
perhaps how I felt.

I cannot read this.
Drinks point to: illegible—
"Not tree dead yet palm."

A return to breath,
the slow distension of bones,
sunlight free of heat.

The lovely lady's
deep in surprising torment—
so lovely, so pale.

A time of goodbyes—
but just for a little while—
the better of whiles.

Two traveling nights,
no haikus to show for them;
arriving: haiku.

The day half-ruined
by one moment of neglect.
But what was that bird?

The year is ending,
and here it hardly matters.
With her, happiness.

So I kept drinking
until most goodbyes were said.
It had rained real rain.

I cannot believe
what photographs are saying:
was I there, ever?

Wherever friends meet,
there is room for surprises,
such as listening.

Lover and poet:
then how to define "poet"?
Dum dum de dum dum

To speak ill of one
who was once so kind to me—
has *he* forgotten?

Breath of affection:
words certainly have a use:
make it ours not theirs—

"theirs" meaning "the words'"—
what are they but viruses
preserving their way?

On the other hand
what—OK—does friendship do?
It preserves "its" way?

Second haiku stoned.
"It is very quiet now.
Eleven o'clock."

No time for haiku!
and no time for reflection!
Stones yard-deep in pool.

A poker haiku:
when confusion starts to reign,
have a sip of wine.

What is essential?
Will I decide every day?
Watch angel trumpets.

The angel trumpet,
the diabolical sax,
and the missing voice.

No haiku tonight.
Haikus undermine haikus.
Tonight, haiku? No!

And some seem better
and some seem beyond salvage;
and "I" drown in words.

A day can go wrong
in the subject's opinion
—the opinion's junk.

So five syllables
then combine themselves with two
before shrinking back.

Haikus are diffic.
Haikus are very diffic.
One haiku is diff.

How a weakened son
Can sow unrest in my heart!
Get the lights working.

My name—hardly mine—
Passes through generations.
Two now. Who are they?

54

A child starts dancing,
His brother then starts dancing.
Dark things keep stalking.

Where is the line drawn
Between commerce and pleasure?
Watch lizards and cats.

My guardian wife
Has left to be guardian
Of others I love.

Where is the other?
Here, among my friends
But harder to name.

Cobbling together
Stuff my other mind tells me.
Vines have no worries.

Where are my glasses?
Right here, under my buttock.
Moths fleeing the rain.

Two horses, no race:
Who crosses the finish line?
Each steps back to see.

Struggling to preserve—
What? This...this...this piece of shit?
Utterly worth it.

Born in New York in 1930, Harry Mathews settled in Europe in 1952 and has since then lived in Spain, Germany, Italy, and (chiefly) France. In 1978 he returned to the United States to teach for several years at Bennington College, Columbia University, and the New School University. Now married to the French writer Marie Chaix, he divides his time between Paris and Key West. When Mathews published his first poems in 1956, he was associated with the so-called New York School of poets, with three of whom (John Ashbery, Kenneth Koch, and James Schuyler) he founded the review *Locus Solus* in 1961. Through his friendship with Georges Perec, he became a member of the Oulipo in 1972. The author of six novels and several collections of poetry, his most recent publications are *Sainte Catherine*, a novella written in French (Éditions P.O.L, 2000), *The Human Country: the Collected Short Stories* (Dalkey Archive Press, 2002), *The Case of the Persevering Maltese: Collected Essays* (Dalkey Archive Press, 2003), *Oulipo Compendium* (co-edited with Alastair Brotchie; Atlas Press and Make Now Press, 2005), and *My Life in CIA: A Chronicle of 1973* (Dalkey Archive Press, 2005).